Make Your Own

PAPER
FARM

Sally and Stewart Walton

SMITHMARK

This edition published in 1994 by
SMITHMARK Publishers Inc.,
16 East 32nd Street,
New York, NY 10016.

1 2 3 4 5 6 7 8 9

SMITHMARK books are available for bulk
purchase for sale promotion and premium use. For
details write or call the manager of special sales,
SMITHMARK Publishers Inc.,
16 East 32nd Street, New York,
NY 10016; (212) 532-6600.

ISBN 0-8317-5964-X

Printed in Belgium.

For Roxy

CREDITS

Editor: Helen Stone
Designer: Jane Molineaux
Additional design by: Rachael Stone
Photographer: Jonathon Pollock
Stylist: Cherry Randell
Diorama artist: John Mac
Crafts inspector: Leslie Thompson
Color separation by: Scantrans Pte. Ltd., Singapore
Printed in Belgium by:
Proost International Book Production

Contents

Introduction   4
Waddling Ducks   6
Fleecy Sheep and Fluffy Lambs   8
Curly-tailed Pigs   10
Grazing Cows   12
Gaggle of Geese   14
Faithful Dogs   16
Scenery to Make   18 & 23
Fold-out Farm Diorama   19
Bearded Goats   24
Cunning Foxes   26
Friendly Horses   28
Clucking Chickens   30
Questions and Answers   32

Introduction

Create your own farm complete with pigs, cows, and goats, using just a few sheets of stiff paper and some basic equipment.

Each project in this book has facts about the animal featured and a full-size pattern for you to trace and transfer onto colored paper. Step-by-step instructions explain how to fold your paper patterns into stunning 3-D models, which you can then decorate.

When you have made the animals, why not make some scenery, using the patterns on pages 18 and 23? Then, open out these pages to reveal an amazing fold-out farm diorama, which is the perfect farmyard setting for your models.

Materials – Each project has a list of materials you will need. Construction paper or thick cartridge paper work best and can be bought from craft or art supply stores. Thin paper makes floppy models and some thick paper is too difficult to cut and fold.

Safety Tips – Be very careful with scissors. When you are not using them, lay them in a safe place with the blades closed. You may wish to use small pointed scissors for some of the smaller cuts; nail scissors are best, but make sure an adult knows you are using them. One or two projects in this book may require the use of a craft knife; always ask an adult to make these cuts for you.

Getting Started – Before you begin any project in this book, read through the steps here to learn the basic techniques.

1. Tracing Patterns

Lay tracing paper onto the animal pattern and hold it firmly in place. Using a soft, sharp pencil, carefully trace the solid outline first and then trace all the fold lines. Take time to get the tracing right. Place your tracing face down onto the paper. Hold the two together with paper clips and firmly redraw over the traced lines to transfer the pencil outline onto the paper.

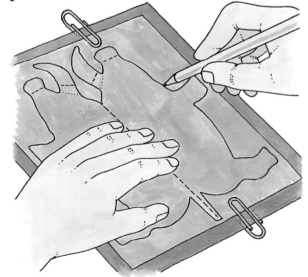

4

2. Cutting Out the Main Shapes

On each pattern, the solid lines are the ones you should cut around and the broken lines are the ones you should fold. Cut out the main shape first and then cut around the details such as beaks, mouths, and ears. Use round-ended scissors where possible and ask an adult to help you if you find some of the smaller cuts difficult.

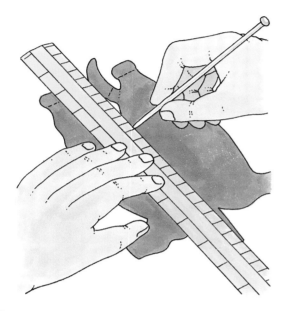

3. Creasing the Fold Lines

Before folding the paper, you should crease all the broken lines to make the folds neat. Lay a ruler along the fold line and lift the paper up against it. Hold it in this position, taking care that the ruler does not slip. Run your finger along the bottom edge where the paper lifts against the ruler. Alternatively, keep the paper flat and draw over the fold line with a knitting needle or a ballpoint pen that no longer works, using a ruler as a guide. Don't press too hard – you only want to dent the paper.

4. Making Folds

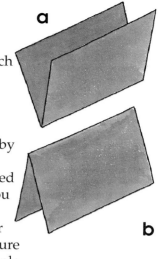

There are two types of folds: valley folds, which dip downward (*a*) or mountain folds, which pop upward (*b*). All downward folds are marked on the pattern by dotted lines and all upward folds are marked with dashed lines. If you have creased the folds accurately, folding your pattern into a 3-D creature should be neat and simple.

5. Decorating Your Model

If you are copying the decorations from the patterns in this book, it is easiest to unfold your model and lay it flat. Colored markers, pencil crayons, or crayons work best. Paint may make the paper buckle. If you are making up your own decorations, you may find it easier to color onto the folded model. Make the decoration as realistic or as wild as you like. For the best results, erase any pencil marks before you begin.

6. Using the Diorama

Pages 19 to 22 contain a fun scene for you to open out and place your finished models in front of. Stand your book upright on a flat surface and fold out the pages of scenery patterns so that they are at right angles with the rest of the book. You may want to use paper clips to keep them in position. Place your paper scenery in front of the diorama and you have a wonderful farmyard setting for your paper animals to roam in.

Waddling Ducks

Ducks spend most of their time floating on ponds and they have special hollow bones which are light, and waterproof feathers that help to keep them dry.

Their feet are webbed with skin flaps between the toes. These act as powerful paddles under the water, which help the duck swim.

When not in the water, ducks like to spend their time on land, waddling around the pond. They eat worms and other insects as well as pondweed.

The drake, or male duck, is usually far more brightly colored than the female hen, although many ducks found on farms are special breeds, which may be all one color.

Follow the instructions on pages 4 and 5 to trace, cut out, and crease a paper duck pattern. Fold it into a 3-D model following the steps opposite. Decorate your duck and sharpen the creases.

You will need
Tracing paper
Pencil
Stiff colored paper
Paper clips
Scissors and ruler
Knitting needle or old
  ballpoint pen
Paper glue
Colored markers, pencil
  crayons, or crayons

FOLDING YOUR DUCK

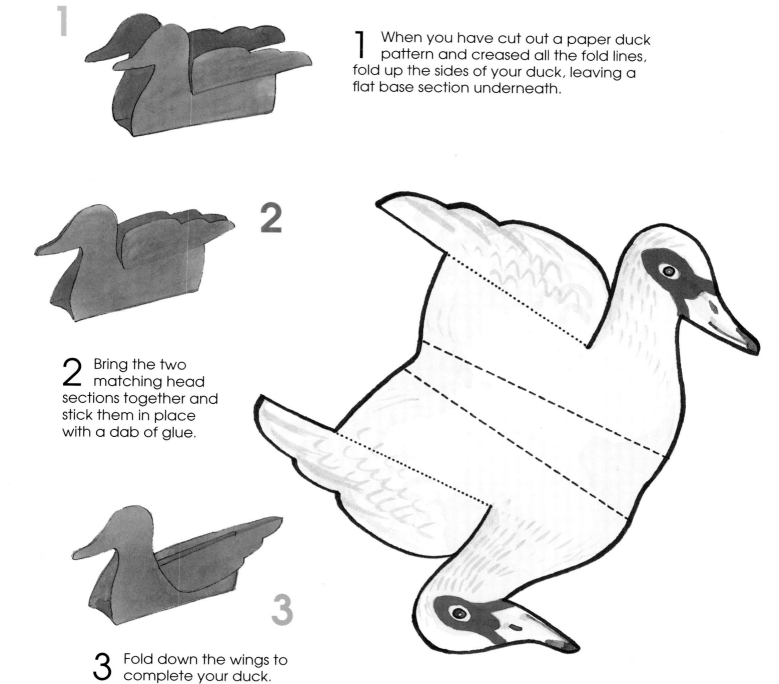

1 When you have cut out a paper duck pattern and creased all the fold lines, fold up the sides of your duck, leaving a flat base section underneath.

2 Bring the two matching head sections together and stick them in place with a dab of glue.

3 Fold down the wings to complete your duck.

Fleecy Sheep and Fluffy Lambs

There are many different types of sheep that are kept on farms for their wool. Sheep are tough animals with thick, wooly fleeces and can live outdoors in all weathers.

The farmer brings his sheep into a sheltered place in the spring when baby lambs are born, but as soon as the lambs are a few weeks old, the sheep go back out to pasture.

During the summer, the flock are sheared. They probably feel very strange and light after losing their heavy woolen coats, but a sheep's fleece grows quickly and, by winter, it will have grown another thick coat to keep it warm.

Follow the instructions on pages 4 and 5 to trace, cut out, and crease a paper pattern. Fold your sheep and lambs following the steps opposite. Lay your models out flat to decorate them and then refold them.

You will need

Tracing paper
Pencil
Thick white cartridge
  paper
Paper clips
Scissors and ruler
Knitting needle or old
  ballpoint pen
Colored markers, pencil
  crayons, or crayons

FOLDING YOUR SHEEP

1

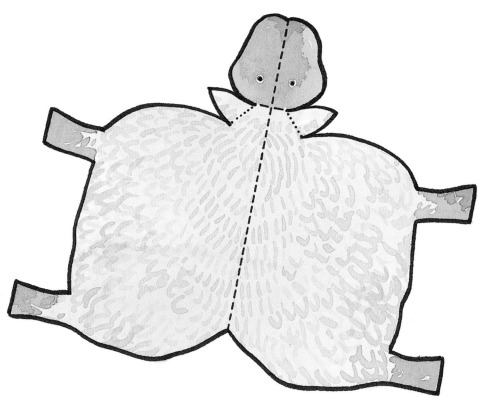

1 Once you have cut out your sheep pattern and creased all the fold lines, make the first fold down the center of the sheep's back.

2

2 Tilt the sheep's head down and fold its ears out.

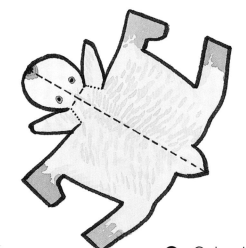

3

3 Cut out and crease a lamb pattern. Fold it down the center. Tilt its head downward and fold the ears so they point up.

9

Curly-tailed Pigs

Pigs have very sensitive noses, known as snouts, which they use for sniffing and digging and sometimes both at the same time. They like to dig for worms to eat as a special treat and, having a big appetite, they can often plow up whole fields looking for juicy worms.

Some farmers let their pigs live outside, but mostly they live in pens known as pigsties where they are fed rich food to make them grow fast.

A mother pig is called a sow and she looks after the young piglets. There may be up to fifteen piglets in one litter and the father pig, the boar, rarely helps her to care for them.

Follow the instructions on pages 4 and 5 to trace, cut out, and crease a paper pig pattern. Fold the pattern into a 3-D model following the steps opposite. Lay the model out flat to decorate it and then refold your pig and sharpen any creases between your fingernails.

You will need
Tracing paper and pencil
Stiff colored paper
Paper clips
Scissors and ruler
Knitting needle or old
  ballpoint pen
Colored markers, pencil
  crayons, or crayons
Paper glue

FOLDING YOUR PIG

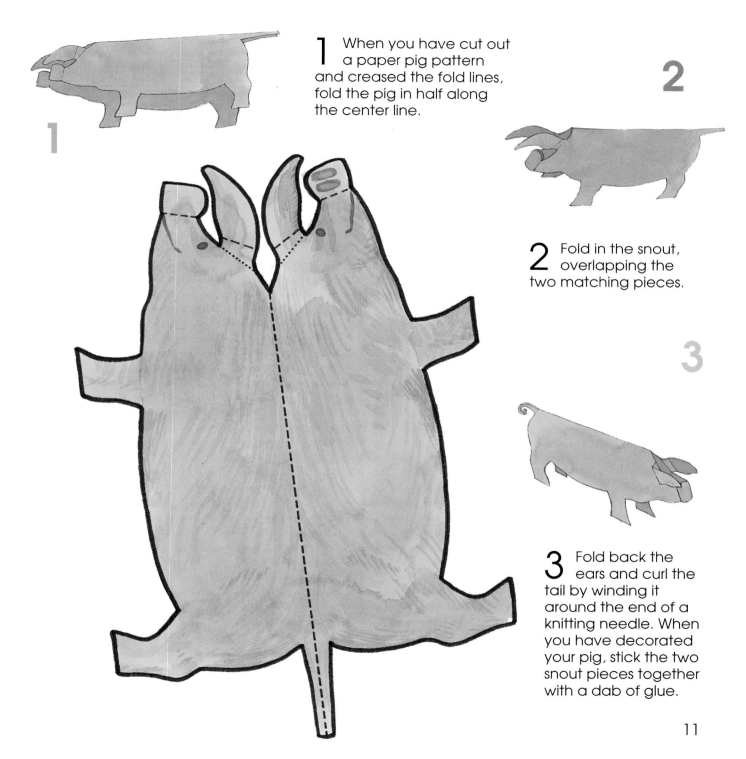

1 When you have cut out a paper pig pattern and creased the fold lines, fold the pig in half along the center line.

2 Fold in the snout, overlapping the two matching pieces.

3 Fold back the ears and curl the tail by winding it around the end of a knitting needle. When you have decorated your pig, stick the two snout pieces together with a dab of glue.

11

Grazing Cows

The cow is a gentle creature and is kept on the farm for the milk it produces. This is the milk that we drink, and it is also used to make butter, cheese, and yogurt.

Cows eat grass, which we cannot digest. A cow's digestive system is very different from ours because it has four stomachs!

Cows are natural herd animals and so they are easy to round up and guide from the pastures to the barn for milking, making them easy animals for the farmer to care for.

Follow the instructions on pages 4 and 5 to trace, cut out, and crease a paper cow pattern. Fold the pattern into a 3-D model following the steps opposite. Lay the cow out flat to decorate it and then refold it, sharpening the creases between your fingernails.

You will need

Tracing paper and pencil
Stiff colored paper
Paper clips
Scissors and ruler
Knitting needle or old
  ballpoint pen
Colored markers, pencil
  crayons, or crayons

FOLDING YOUR COW

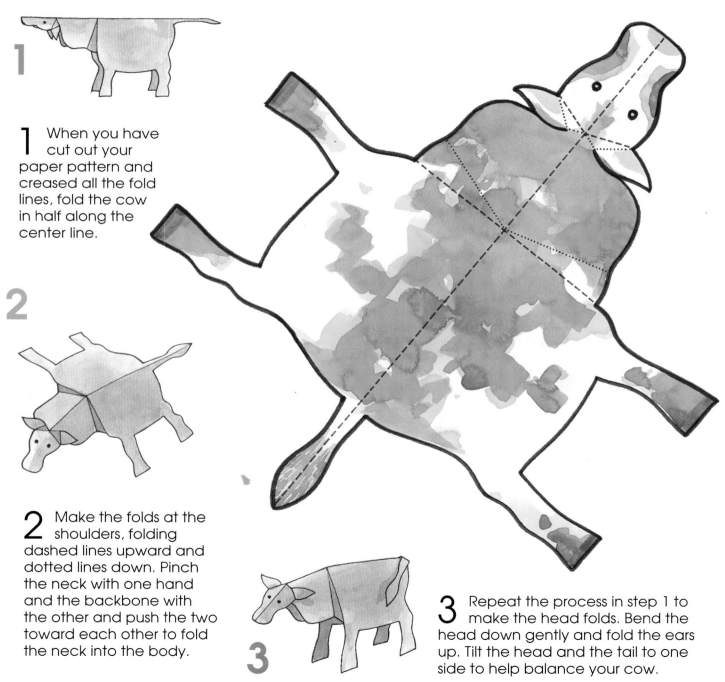

1 When you have cut out your paper pattern and creased all the fold lines, fold the cow in half along the center line.

2 Make the folds at the shoulders, folding dashed lines upward and dotted lines down. Pinch the neck with one hand and the backbone with the other and push the two toward each other to fold the neck into the body.

3 Repeat the process in step 1 to make the head folds. Bend the head down gently and fold the ears up. Tilt the head and the tail to one side to help balance your cow.

13

Gaggle of Geese

Geese can be found in many farmyards and are one of the biggest farm birds.

They like to splash in the water, but spend much of their time on land, grazing on grass as cows do. Wild geese fly south in the winter in huge flocks to avoid the cold weather, but farm geese are happy to stay at home, waddling around the farm feeling important.

Farmers often keep geese as watchdogs because they can be quite fierce and honk and hiss loudly if a stranger approaches. If challenged, they will attack using their strong wings and will peck with their beaks.

Follow the instructions on pages 4 and 5 to trace, cut out, and crease a paper goose pattern. Fold the pattern into a 3-D model following the steps opposite. Lay the model out flat to decorate it and then refold it, sharpening the creases between your fingernails.

You will need
Tracing paper and pencil
Stiff colored paper
Paper clips
Scissors and ruler
Knitting needle or old
  ballpoint pen
Colored markers, pencil
  crayons, or crayons

FOLDING YOUR GOOSE

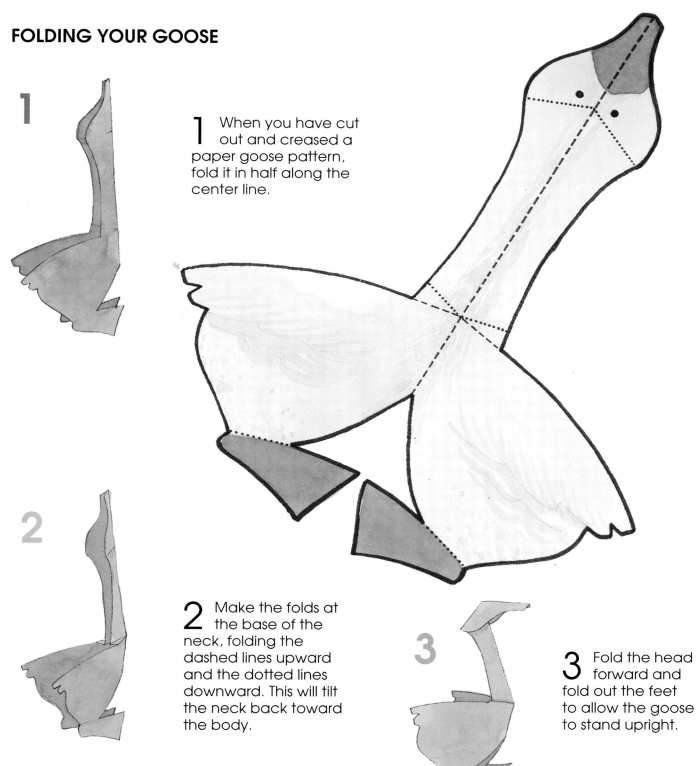

1 When you have cut out and creased a paper goose pattern, fold it in half along the center line.

2 Make the folds at the base of the neck, folding the dashed lines upward and the dotted lines downward. This will tilt the neck back toward the body.

3 Fold the head forward and fold out the feet to allow the goose to stand upright.

Faithful Dogs

Dogs have been keeping people company for many thousands of years. However, the farm dog is not a pet – it plays a very important role on the farm.

A sheep farmer can control his large flocks and let them roam over the hills if he has a pair of sheep dogs to help him. The dogs will search for any lost sheep and round up the flocks following hand signals, whistles, and shouts from their master.

The farm dog's work doesn't stop at the end of the day. By night, he acts as a guard and uses his good sense of smell and hearing to detect foxes and other wild animals that could attack the farmer's chickens.

Follow the instructions on pages 4 and 5 to trace, cut out, and crease a paper dog pattern. Fold the pattern into a 3-D model following the steps opposite. Lay the model out flat to decorate it and then refold it, sharpening the creases between your fingernails.

You will need
Tracing paper and pencil
Stiff colored paper
Paper clips
Scissors and ruler
Knitting needle or old
  ballpoint pen
Colored markers, pencil
  crayons, or crayons

Scenery to Make

Simple foliage and fences are easy to make and can be used to create exciting settings for your paper farm animals.

Follow the instructions on pages 4 and 5 to transfer these patterns onto colored paper. You can make longer lengths of grass and fencing by tracing the same pattern several times, joining one onto the next.

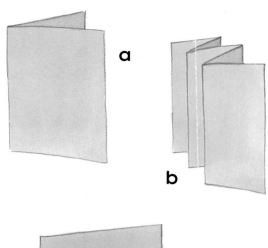

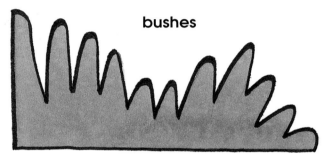

bushes

Fold long lengths of bush or fence patterns concertina-style.

FOLDING YOUR FOLIAGE

There are three main ways to fold the scenery. Once you have traced the shapes, transferred them onto colored paper, and cut them out, fold the patterns in one of the following ways:

(a) Fold the shape in half down the center to make it stand upright.

(b) Fold the shape backward and forward, concertina-style, to make rows of grass or fencing.

(c) Make one or more right-angled folds to form a box shape for bales of hay or bushes.

fence

tufts of grass

18

FOLDING YOUR DOG

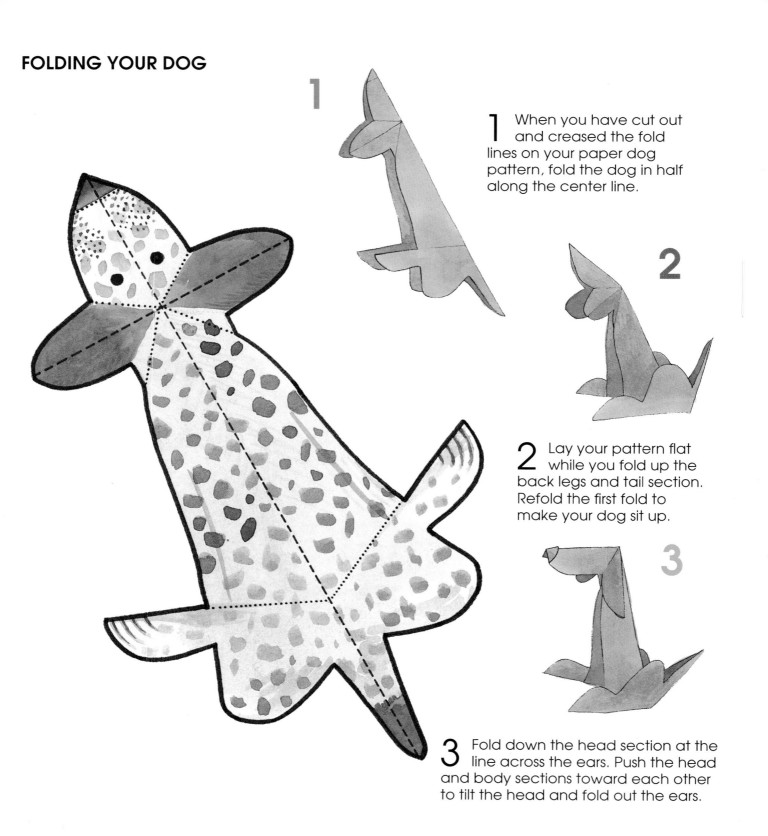

1 When you have cut out and creased the fold lines on your paper dog pattern, fold the dog in half along the center line.

2 Lay your pattern flat while you fold up the back legs and tail section. Refold the first fold to make your dog sit up.

3 Fold down the head section at the line across the ears. Push the head and body sections toward each other to tilt the head and fold out the ears.

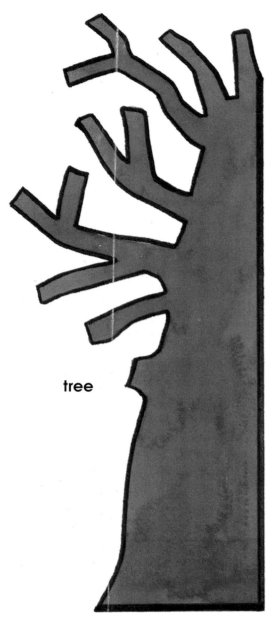

tree

To make a bale of hay, transfer a row of four joining hay patterns onto colored paper and fold them into a box shape.

straw and hay

grass

To make the tree, fold a sheet of colored paper in half. Transfer the pattern onto the folded paper, keeping the straight edge of the tree shape against the fold. Cut out the shape you have drawn and unfold the paper to reveal your tree.

23

FOLDING YOUR GOAT

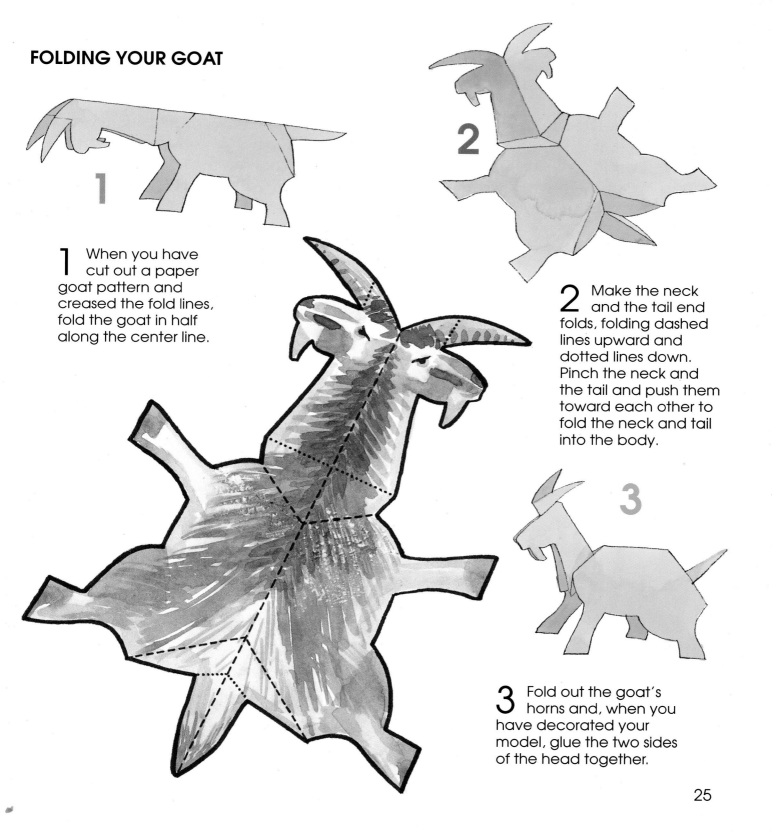

1 When you have cut out a paper goat pattern and creased the fold lines, fold the goat in half along the center line.

2 Make the neck and the tail end folds, folding dashed lines upward and dotted lines down. Pinch the neck and the tail and push them toward each other to fold the neck and tail into the body.

3 Fold out the goat's horns and, when you have decorated your model, glue the two sides of the head together.

25

Cunning Foxes

The fox is related to the dog but, as a wild animal, it is far more sly and clever. The fox has excellent hearing and its big pointed ears can swivel around to identify the smallest or most distant sounds.

A fox's sense of smell is much stronger than our own and it uses it to sniff out danger and food.

The fox has strong legs which enable it to run fast and a big bushy tail, which gives it good balance.

Foxes will eat almost any meat and will also eat mushrooms and fruit. Many farmers see the fox as an enemy because at night it will attack lambs and chickens for food.

Follow the instructions on pages 4 and 5 to trace, cut out, and crease a paper fox pattern. Fold the pattern into a 3-D model following the steps opposite. Lay the model flat to decorate it and then refold it and sharpen the creases between your fingernails.

You will need
Tracing paper and pencil
Stiff colored paper
Paper clips
Scissors and ruler
Knitting needle or old ballpoint pen
Colored markers, pencil crayons, or crayons
White paint and paintbrush

FOLDING YOUR FOX

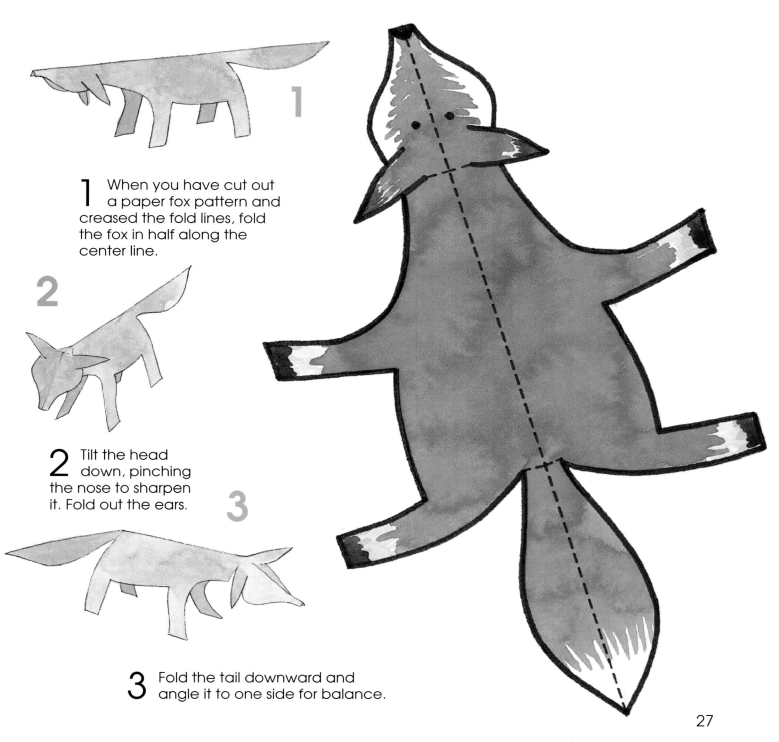

1 When you have cut out a paper fox pattern and creased the fold lines, fold the fox in half along the center line.

2 Tilt the head down, pinching the nose to sharpen it. Fold out the ears.

3 Fold the tail downward and angle it to one side for balance.

Friendly Horses

In days gone by, horses worked hard on the farm. They pulled the plows in the fields and carried the farmer to town, pulling carts and carrying heavy loads.

Today, modern machinery works the farmland and the horses have a much easier life. In some places, horses are still used to round up cattle and pull carts, but mostly they are just ridden for pleasure.

Horses are housed in stables and eat hay, grass, and oats.

Follow the instructions on pages 4 and 5 to trace, cut out, and crease a paper horse pattern. Fold it into a 3-D model following the steps opposite. Lay the model out flat to decorate it and then refold it and sharpen any creases between your fingernails.

You will need
Tracing paper and pencil
Stiff colored paper
Paper clips
Scissors and ruler
Knitting needle or old ballpoint pen
Colored markers, pencil crayons, or crayons

FOLDING YOUR HORSE

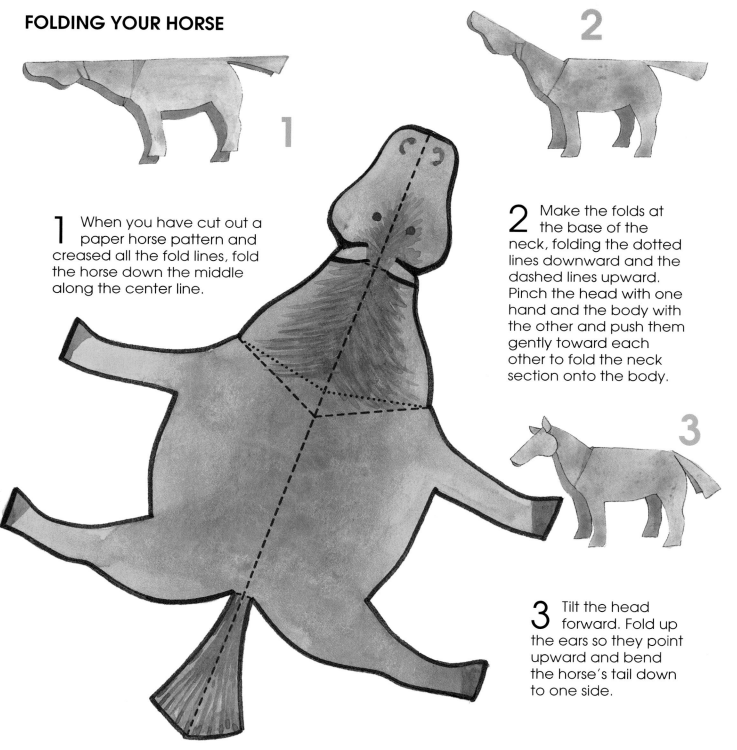

1 When you have cut out a paper horse pattern and creased all the fold lines, fold the horse down the middle along the center line.

2 Make the folds at the base of the neck, folding the dotted lines downward and the dashed lines upward. Pinch the head with one hand and the body with the other and push them gently toward each other to fold the neck section onto the body.

3 Tilt the head forward. Fold up the ears so they point upward and bend the horse's tail down to one side.

Clucking Chickens

The chickens found in the farmyard today have their ancestors in the wildfowl of India which were tamed a long time ago. There are hundreds of different breeds which come in all shapes, colors, and sizes. Some lay small speckled eggs and others lay large white or brown ones.

They live happily in the farmyard, pecking at the ground and scratching for insects and worms in the daytime. At night, they roost on perches in the henhouse and lay their eggs in straw-filled nests. If a hen is broody it means that she is sitting on a clutch of eggs to hatch them. It takes about three weeks for the baby chicks to hatch.

Follow the instructions on pages 4 and 5 to trace, cut out, and crease a paper chicken pattern. Fold the shape into a 3-D model following the steps opposite. Decorate your model and sharpen the folds between your fingernails.

You will need

Tracing paper and pencil
Stiff colored paper
Paper clips
Scissors and ruler
Knitting needle or old ballpoint pen
Paper glue
Colored markers, pencil crayons,
  or crayons

FOLDING YOUR CHICKEN

1 When you have cut out a paper chicken pattern and creased all the fold lines, fold up the chicken's sides, leaving a flat base section underneath.

2 Bring together the two matching head sections and stick them together with a dab of glue.

3 Fold down the wings at right angles to the body and push the single tail feather in between the two tail feathers on the opposite side.

Questions and Answers

When you have made all the models, test your knowledge of the animals featured by answering the questions in this quiz. The answers can be found in this book. Turn the page upside down to check your score.

1. What do horses eat?

2. Which animals have been keeping people company for thousands of years?

3. What are baby goats called?

4. Which wild animal is related to the dog?

5. How many stomachs does a cow have?

6. Which animal's diet includes meat, mushrooms, and fruit?

7. At which time of year are lambs born?

8. What do pigs eat as a treat?

9. Which creature, other than the dog, guards the farmyard?

10. In which three ways does a shepherd signal to his sheep dog?

11. What is the very special type of goat's wool called?

12. Name three milk products.

13. Why do geese fly south in winter?

14. What is special about a duck's feet that help it swim?

15. How many piglets can a sow have in one litter?

Answers

1. Grass and hay. 2. Dogs. 3. Kids. 4. The fox. 5. Four. 6. The fox. 7. The spring. 8. Worms. 9. The goose. 10. Hand signals, whistles, and shouts. 11. Cashmere. 12. Butter, cheese, and yogurt. 13. To avoid the cold weather. 14. They are webbed. 15. Up to fifteen.